Oh, the Wonder of
His Word

Ghost Writer:
LAURA RUSSELL SIMPSON

WESTBOW
PRESS®
A DIVISION OF THOMAS NELSON
& ZONDERVAN

Scripture taken from the King James Version of the Bible.

WestBow Press books may be ordered through booksellers or by contacting:

WestBow Press
A Division of Thomas Nelson & Zondervan
1663 Liberty Drive
Bloomington, IN 47403
www.westbowpress.com
1 (866) 928-1240

ISBN: 978-1-9736-0411-2 (sc)
ISBN: 978-1-9736-0410-5 (e)

Print information available on the last page.

WestBow Press rev. date: 10/12/2017

DEDICATION

The writings in this book are dedicated to the glory of Almighty God! May He be high and lifted up! And to the glory of His Son, Jesus Christ, the Savior of the world! May He, too, be high and lifted up! And to the Holy Spirit, the Spirit of the living God, the One True God! The One who lives in those who are His and seals us to the day of redemption! The One who brings us to salvation, the One who teaches us the truths of God, the One who guides, comforts, and keeps us! And the One who reveals the Father to us!!! All praises be to the Father, Son and Holy Ghost!!!

Alleluia!!!

Laura Russell Simpson 8-7-17

FROM THE AUTHOR

If you are reading this book and have also read any of the others I have published, you will see that some of the writings are included in each of them. I have followed God's lead in doing this. According to His will and my heartfelt desire, God's plan of salvation, with Jesus as the only Way, will always be presented first. Then there will be a few others that are also included. However, each book has new writings and teachings. If you are blessed as you read God's Word to us, then I am greatly blessed!

TO THE READER

Genesis 1:3 And God said(spoke), Let there be light, and there was light.

Genesis 1:9 And God said(spoke), Let the waters under the heaven be gathered together unto one place, and let dry land appear: and it was so.

Genesis 1:11 And God said(spoke) Let the earth bring forth grass, the herb yielding seed, and the fruit tree yielding fruit after his kind, whose seed is in itself, upon the earth: and it was so.

Genesis 1:14&15 And God said(spoke), Let there be lights in the firmament of the heaven to divide the day from the night: and let them be for signs, and for seasons, and for days and years. And let them be for lights in the firmament of the heaven to give light upon the earth: and it was so.

Genesis 1:20 And God said(spoke), Let the waters bring forth abundantly the moving creature that hath life, and fowl that may fly above the earth in the open firmament of heaven.

Genesis 1: 24 And God said(spoke), Let the earth bring forth the living creature after his kind, cattle, and creeping thing, and beast of the earth after his kind: and it was so.

Genesis 1:26&27 And God said(spoke), Let us make man in our image, after our likeness: and let them have dominion over the fish of the sea, and over the fowl of the air, and over the cattle, and over all the earth, and over every creeping thing that creepeth upon the earth. So, God created man in His own image, in the image of God created He him: male and female created He first.

Genesis 2:1 Thus the heavens and earth were finished, and all the host of them.

Genesis 2:2 And on the seventh day God ended His work which He had made, and He rested on the seventh day from all His work which He had made.

In the first chapter of the book of Genesis, the first book of God's written Word to us, we are awestruck by the wonder of His Word as we read. God literally spoke the world and all in it into existence. This brings to our attention the power of the Word of our God. Journey with me as we read and discover for ourselves some of these awesome wonders. You will be greatly blessed!

THE MESSAGE OF THE CROSS AND BEYOND

From One Who Said "Yes!"

If you have a void in your life that you cannot seem to fill, or maybe you feel you have no purpose, or maybe you have lost hope; then I would like to tell you about One you may not know, who can answer all your needs. May I introduce you to the One I speak about? His name is Jesus. His gift is free to you, but not to Him. His gift to you cost Him His life. Did you know this Jesus loves you so much that He willingly died a horrible, shameful death on a wooden cross at a place called Calvary in order to provide a way for you to be forgiven for your sins? And before He was nailed to that cross, He was beaten beyond recognition. Blood ran down His head and face from a crown of thorns. He was mocked and spit upon. Only vinegar and gall was offered Him to drink. The only thing He was guilty of was loving all people, healing and delivering multitudes, and revealing God, His Father, to a world who rejected Him. He hung there for hours before died. And did you know He is the only Way of salvation? For Jesus, Himself, said He is the Way, the Truth, and the Life. No man comes to the Father, but by Him (John 14:6). He tells you, if you believe there is any other way to Heaven, then His death was in vain. His shed blood is the only way you can have forgiveness for your sins. He paid your penalty for you with His life. How great a love is that! If you want forgiveness for your sins, and an eternal home in Heaven, and blessings beyond measure; then just pray a simple prayer. It does not have to be eloquent. First, admit to Him that you are a sinner. Confess your sins and invite Him into your heart to live and reign as Savior and Lord. At that very moment, His free gift is yours. And you only have to ask once. How easy is that? Then believe it by faith. If you have done this, you have just entered into a wonderful relationship with the One True God. You now have God's very own Spirit living in you. It is the work of the Holy Spirit that will bring you blessings beyond measure. Your journey with Jesus has now begun. Once He has touched you, your life will never, ever, be the same. It will truly be an awesome experience. And it is the most important decision you will ever make. Your life beyond the Cross will bring these and more: Joy Unspeakable (1 Peter 1:8), Healing (1 Peter 2:24), Freedom (John 8:36), An Exciting Life (John 10:10), Peace Instead Of Anxiety (Philippians (4:7), Strength In Weakness (2 Corinthians 12:9), Love For Others (Galatians 5:22), Hope (Romans 15:13), Guidance (Isaiah 58:1), Happiness (Proverbs 16:20), Help In Times Of Affliction (Hebrews 4:16), Comfort (2 Corinthians 1:3&4), An Eternal Home In Heaven (John 10:28), Answered Prayers (John 14:13&14), Deliverance (2Chronicles 20:17), Wisdom And Knowledge (Ephesians 1:17). I want to close with this: None of us deserve what God gives us when we are saved. It truly is His grace. As we walk in the power of His Holy Spirit, His grace will grow us. Our life in Him will truly be an abundant one. We just have to yield our hearts to Him daily. I tell you from my personal experience with Him, when He touched me, my life changed drastically. I simply must share with all the good news of His gospel message. This gospel message is not to be kept a secret!

Alleluia!!!

In His Great Love, Laura Russell Simpson 8-10-15

AT THE BEGINNING OF A NEW DAY

God is always calling us to a greater place, a greater relationship with Him, a greater faith, a greater walk, a greater peace, a greater revelation, a greater vision, a greater knowledge, a greater truth, a greater growth and maturity, a greater joy, a greater victory, a greater power, a greater path, a greater understanding, a greater experience, and a greater ending!!!

Alleluia!!!

Ghost Writer For God
Laura Russell Simpson

TRUTH OR CONSEQUENCES

John 14:6

Jesus saith unto him, I am the Way, the TRUTH, and the Life: no man comes unto the Father, but by Me.

There are many who are on a quest seeking the truth. The fact is that the truth is not something we seek. The truth is Someone we seek. And His name is Jesus!

Here Jesus tells us clearly that He is the Truth. And He, being the Truth, speaks three truths to us. First, He is the only Way of salvation. Second, He declares that He is the Truth. And third He says that it is only through Him that any man can come to the Father. There are some who reject these words of Jesus and even reject the Word of God as written in the Bible, but that does not make God's Word, with Jesus' words here, any less true. It is these same ones who are seeking to fill that God-shaped void inside them, but are blinded by the enemy of our souls. He(Satan) sends them out looking for something when the truth is, that which they seek is a person. Again, that One is Jesus. Only at the cross, through the shed blood of Jesus, are blinded eyes opened. Those who continue to reject Jesus as the only way of salvation and the only way to our heavenly Father will one day, when they step into eternity, meet the Truth face to face. They will stand before Jesus and hear His Words, depart from Me, I knew you not. And they will go on to spend eternity in a place prepared for them called Hell. And that, my friends, is Forever! For those who may be on this quest seeking the truth, turn to Jesus and ask Him to reveal Himself to you. In seeking, you will find Him.

In my seeking, more of The Truth/Jesus, I found numerous scriptures where inserting the name of Jesus in place of the word truth brought new light upon these words. Please allow me to share some of these with you. Jesus literally walks off the pages of God's written Word! Along with the scriptures given, I have inserted the name Jesus with the word truth.

John 5:33

Ye sent unto us John, and he bare witness unto the truth(Jesus). Remember here that John, the Baptist, was sent by God to proclaim that Jesus was the Christ. John pointed us to Jesus/Someone/ the Truth, and also the truth(Something), that He was the Christ.

Psalm 51

In David's Psalm of Repentance, he says, Behold, Thou desires truth(Jesus), who would one day come, in the inward parts: and in the hidden part Thou shall make me to know wisdom. These words of David, of course, were written long before the birth of Christ. However, I believe inside every person there is a desire to fill the void that only Jesus can fill. We just have to know the Way of that filling. Important here, is sharing the gospel of Jesus Christ by those of us who belong to Him with those who have never heard. I can hear the heart of David as he wrote these beautiful words. It seems that he was seeking the One yet to come and his truths which lead us all to wisdom.

Psalm 117:2

His truth(Jesus) endureth forever.

We know that Jesus was in the beginning and will reign as King of Kings and Lord of Lords throughout eternity. And that is surely forever!

Psalm 119:30

I have chosen the way of truth(Jesus).

Turn your thoughts toward the New Testament. I ask you, what is your choice? What is the way you have chosen? Is your choice Someone(Jesus) or something(false truth)?

Zechariah 8:16

Speak every man truth to his neighbor.

Through the words of Zechariah, we hear speaking truthful words. But again, looking to the New Testament, we hear of sharing Jesus with others.

John 17:19

.........that they also might be sanctified through the truth(Jesus).

The truth here is that we are sanctified through Jesus. Again, the word truth and the name Jesus are interchangeable.

John 18:37

Everyone that is of the truth(Jesus) heareth My voice.

His Words are so very clear. If we are His, yes, we hear our Savior's voice. He says this again when He speaks of being the Good Shepherd. He says, My sheep hear My voice.

John 8:32

You shall know the truth(Jesus), and the truth(Jesus) shall make you free.

It is this One, Jesus, the Truth, who sets us free from the sins which so easily beset us, and the bondages that imprison us.

2 John 2:2

……..for the truth's(Jesus')sake, which dwelleth in us, and shall be with us forever.

It is through the presence of His Holy Spirit that Jesus lives in us and seals us to the day of redemption.

John 17:17

Thy Word is truth(Jesus).

This verse reminds us of Jesus being the Living Word.

John 18:38

Pilate saith unto Him, What is truth?

So often we read or hear of those who ask this very question. What is truth? So very interesting here are the words of Jesus just before Pilate asked this question. Jesus had just said, everyone that is of the truth(Jesus) heareth My voice. Jesus' Words point to Himself, not something!

2 Timothy 3:7

..........ever learning, and never able to come to the knowledge of the truth(Jesus).

These Words take our thoughts, especially to the academic world. Those who esteem themselves as intellects, studying, researching, thinking themselves to be wise and knowledgeable. They seek the truth as something. It is this very thing that will keep them from coming to the knowledge of the truth(Jesus).

For Further Study:

2 Timothy 2:15

James 5:19

1 John 3:19

1 John 5:6

John 16:13

Ephesians 4:15

Galatians 2:5

2 Thessalonians 2:12

In closing, heavenly Father, we ask You to help us to continue seeking more of Jesus(Someone), and more of His truths(Something). And we pray for those who are still seeking. Open blind eyes to The Truth!

Alleluia!!!

Ghost Writer For God
Laura Russell Simpson 7-30-17

JOHN, THE BAPTIST'S WORDS MADE PERSONAL

John 3:30

HE(Jesus) must increase, but I must decrease.

John the Baptist's words ring in my ears as I recall this passage of scripture. For the first time God made these words personal. What I heard from Him was this. I, too, must decrease, and Jesus must increase in me. Each new day He gives us, if we walk with Him, we must put self aside and follow our Lord. And as we follow Him closely, He(Jesus) will increase in us. Being the Light of the World, Jesus' light will shine through us. This Light in us, which can come only through Him, will draw those who live in darkness to us, giving us opportunities to share the great and awesome love of God and His way of salvation, which comes only through His Son, Jesus Christ. The Holy Spirit, in those who are His, will give His words of encouragement to those who are discouraged. He will guide us in the paths of His choice, not ours. He will open doors and close doors. Being the Living Word, He(Jesus) will cause the Word to live in us. But this comes through reading God's Word and knowing the power and truth of it. The more of God's Word we know and practice, the more we will decrease, and the more Jesus will increase in us. Crucifying self, daily, even moment by moment, and allowing Jesus to reign and rule will produce in us, too, true joy, no matter our circumstances. We will experience true peace, that peace which surpasses all understanding. We will have His strength in our weaknesses. We will see answers to our prayers as we set our love upon Him (Psalm 91:14&15). His blessings, which come in many forms, will be heaped upon us as we follow Jesus(decrease) and allow Him(Jesus) to increase. In reading this passage of scripture in John 3, you will hear more beautiful words spoken by John, the Baptist. Just before he says he must decrease and Jesus increase, John says that his joy is fulfilled. Why? Because John says he has heard Jesus' voice. Let us first, like John, know true joy as we hear our Lord, Jesus Christ's voice and then allow Him to increase in us.

Alleluia!!!

Laura Russell Simpson 7-15-17

HOW MANY MIRACLES DO WE MISS?

Mark 6:45-54

And straightway He constrained His disciples to get into the ship, and to go to the other side before unto Bethsaida, while He sent away the people. And when He had sent them away, He departed into a mountain to pray. And when even was come, the ship was in the midst of the sea, and He alone on the land. And He saw them toiling in rowing, for the wind was contrary unto them: and about the fourth watch of the night He cometh unto them, walking upon the sea, and would have passed by them. But when they saw Him walking upon the sea, they supposed it had been a spirit, and cried out: for they all saw Him, and were troubled. And immediately He talked with them, and saith unto them, Be of good cheer: it is I; be not afraid. And He went up unto them into the ship; and the wind ceased: and they were sore amazed in themselves beyond measure, and wondered. For they considered not the miracle of the loaves for their heart was hardened. And when they had passed over, they came into the land of Gennesaret, and drew to the shore. And when they were come out of the ship, straightway they knew Him.

Before revealing to us, in this passage, all our Father wants us to see, He first wants us to see that in the preceding verses Jesus has just performed a great miracle. He has just fed five thousand people with five loaves of bread and two fishes. And His disciples were very much a part of this miracle. He gave the commands, and they obeyed. Then immediately after this miracle, Jesus puts them into a ship and sends them to the other side to Bethsaida. Notice here that He obviously did not need their help. He, himself, sent the people away. After then Jesus goes into a mountain to pray. When I read this, I asked, what did you pray to Your Father? This thought intrigues me. I just have to wonder what They talked about when He prayed. Next, as dark approaches, the ship is now in the midst of the sea, and the verse says that Jesus was alone on the land. Verse 48 tells us He saw them struggling to row the ship against the wind. And then about the fourth watch, He comes to them walking on the sea. It also says He was going to pass on by them. I wonder why? A great lesson here for us is to know first that God sends us, also, into storms in our lives. Remember His Words. Many are the afflictions of the righteous, but He delivers them out of them all (Psalm 34:19). But as with the disciples, He sees and knows when we are in the midst of our storms. Jesus is watching as we, too, struggle against our own winds. Next, the scripture says, Jesus came out to them about the fourth watch of the night. And He comes to them walking on the water. The fourth watch of the night is the last part of the night, so He did not hurry to help them. He let them struggle awhile. And then comes one of His greatest miracles, walking on the water. Look what happens. They did not even recognize Him. They cry out in fear. Jesus addresses this with great words of comfort. Be of good cheer: it is I, be not afraid. He then gets into the ship with them and the wind stops. At this point, they are amazed, beyond measure the verse says. But they still did not recognize Him. Why? Because they had not "considered" the miracle of the loaves, because their hearts were hardened. Obviously, they did not even remember the miracle they had just experienced. Now, I ask you, my friends,

17

does that sound familiar? I will quickly admit it sure sounds familiar to me! God has sent me into many storms trying to teach me about Himself and who Jesus is. Also, to strengthen my faith in Him. These verses, given to us in God's written Word, let us know Jesus sees us in our struggles and always comes to help us, too. But sometimes it may be the "fourth watch" of our night. Again, He is trying to teach us to trust and wait on Him to reveal His help. Each of these times are "our miracles". Do we remember when the next storm comes, or are we like the disciples and do not even "consider" our miracles? So, I ask myself and you, my friends, how many miracles do we miss? And in our miracles, do we remember, or even know, His words of comfort? Sometimes I am so busy shrieking with fear that I do not hear His voice or recognize His presence with me. Forgive me, Lord, for my hard heart. In the last two verses, we learn that when they reached the shore and got out of the boat, they recognized Him. But they had missed two major miracles, the feeding of the five thousand with five loaves of bread and the two fishes, and Jesus coming to help them walking on the water. In closing I, again, ask myself, how many miracles have I missed in my lifetime. And beyond that how much greater my faith would be if I had remembered these times and let them grow me spiritually. Thank You, my Father, for Your awesome patience and grace.

Alleluia!!!

Ghost Writer For God
Laura Russell Simpson 3-6-17

Take heart, my friends, Jesus sees you in your storm struggling. He is coming! It may be awhile, but He is coming!!! And when He does come, do not miss your miracle!

GOD'S REMINDER TO US

He is all we will ever need, because He is everything we will ever need!!!

Alleluia!!!

Ghost Writer For God: Laura Russell Simpson 2-28-1

THE GIFT OF GIVING

Acts 20:35

From God's Heart to Ours. Giving. Our heavenly Father set the supreme example for each of us. He gave the ultimate gift of His Son, Jesus, to die for our sins so that we might be forgiven and have an eternal home in Heaven. And, also, that we could have a personal relationship with our Father. Then Jesus gave His ultimate gift by giving His life, the only Way of salvation, for our life. He left us with His Words: it is more blessed to give than to receive. God's gift to us of giving is nothing short of a miracle. When we obey His Words, something happens in our hearts. And what happens in us is not about getting. It is God's blessing in our hearts, which produces joy, a love that only God can give us, unending pleasure, and a desire to give more. Is that surprising? Well, look at what causes this to grow? More giving! As we give more our hearts are blessed more. Then we experience more joy, more pleasures, and more of God's love to share, which fills us to an overflow. With all of these comes more and more desire to give more. The gift of giving, which comes from our heavenly Father, is not about money. We can give in many ways. Certainly, money is one thing. We need to give to send the gospel message out to a dying world. But our gifts can be a tray of baked goodies, a call or a card to someone who needs a word of encouragement, a visit to someone who is lonely, a smile, a thank you note instead of a text to someone who has done something nice for you, and not the least, sharing Jesus and the love of God with one God places in your path. When we do these kinds of things, we experience a heart full of the love of God and, again, full of His blessings upon us. In the end we give our ultimate, which is sharing the awesome love of our Father and God, and our Savior, Jesus, with those He blessedly places in our daily paths.

Heavenly Father, help us not to miss Your gift of giving to us. And more so, help us not reject it, thus missing Your great blessings, which is what we receive as we give. If we do miss this, we will truly miss a great miracle from You in our hearts!

Alleluia!!!

Ghost Writer For God
Laura Russell Simpson 6-20-17

It is not about what we get. It is about what happens in our hearts.

THE PRIVILEGE OF PRAYER

Psalm 91:14&15

Because he hath set his love upon Me, therefore, will I deliver him: I will set him on high, because he hath known My name. He shall call upon Me, and I will answer him: I will be with him in trouble; I will deliver him and honor him.

How appropriate that on this Monday of Holy Week, God would bring again, these verses of scripture to my mind. I have read these many times and thanked Him for such wonderful promises, but this day He has revealed another message. Out of these today, He has shown me the privilege of prayer. I ask myself, as I write, and all who read this, if we fully comprehend that when we offer up our prayers, we are coming into the presence of the Almighty. And He tells us to come boldly. Thank You, Father. We are coming to the One who holds the universe He created, and all in it. We are coming to the One who holds all power. We are coming to the One alone who is Holy. We are coming to the great I AM! And the privilege of coming to Him with our requests began the moment Jesus gave up His life, after shedding His royal, holy blood. At that very moment, the veil in the temple was torn from top to bottom, thus opening up our access into the Holy of Holies. Our great High Priest, the Lord Jesus Christ, gave us access to the very presence of God. I ask you, my friends, is this not an awesome privilege? Our loving Father, who cannot look upon sin provided us a way, the only Way, which came through the shed blood of His only beloved Son, the Lord Jesus Christ. My thoughts go toward how a Holy God could even want sinful man to come into His presence. The answer is LOVE!!! The love of God who desires a relationship with each of us, a God who desires to help us, a God who wants us to ask and then answer. These verses reveal all this to us and so much more.

Thank You, Father, for loving us so much that You would provide a Way for us to come boldly into

Your presence with our prayers, and thank You, Jesus, for the sacrifice of Your life to make it all possible.

Alleluia!!!

Ghost Writer For God
Laura Russell Simpson 4-10-17

MAKING PSALM 100 PERSONAL

Offer This Psalm To Him Today

Father, I make a joyful noise to You this day! I serve You with gladness! I come before Your presence with singing! I KNOW that You are God! That You are Lord! I know that You made me, not me, myself! I am one in Your family. I am a sheep in Your pasture. Today I enter through Your gates with great thanksgiving, and I come into Your courts with great praises! I am so very thankful to You, and I bless Your awesome and holy name! You alone are good. Your mercy is everlasting. Your truth alone continues to endure to All generations!

Alleluia!!!

Ghost Writer
Laura Russell Simpson 3-24-16

BEAUTIFUL INSIGHT ON THE GREAT COMMISSION

Psalm 1:3

And he shall be like a tree planted by the rivers of water, that bringeth forth his fruit in his season; his leaf, also, shall not wither; and whatsoever he doeth shall prosper.

Proverbs 11:30

The fruit of the righteous is a tree of life, and he that winneth souls is wise.

In these verses God again shows us the significance of His choice of the use of the tree in His Word. In Psalm 1:1 God is addressing the godly. In Psalm 1:2 He describes the godly as those who delight in His Word., those who meditate on His Word day and night. And in verse 3 He says the godly will be like a tree planted by the rivers of water. These waters He shows us here are waters that as a river continue to flow, always giving the tree what it needs to live. And remember the Words of Jesus as He spoke and said, out of His belly shall flow rivers of living water(John 7:38). This water will always flow, giving those who are truly His, the sustenance we need to live. And hear Him tell us we are planted. Our roots grow deep. We are established, firmly planted. Then, as trees, we will bring forth our fruit, which comes from the work of His Holy Spirit in and through us. And He shows us, too, that we have a season in which our fruit is on us as a tree. Our leaves will never wither because we are continually watered by the "river" we are so firmly planted by. Lastly, in this passage God tells us He will honor us and reward us by His prospering us in whatever we do. How beautiful are these, His Words, to the godly. In Proverbs 11:30 He, again, speaks of the tree and its fruit. It is the fruit of the godly which becomes a tree of life. If He declares us godly, our fruit, which again comes in and through us by His Holy Spirit, will hang on our branches for those who are hungry to pluck and eat from. And this tree, here, is also being sustained by the rivers of living water, because we, too, are rooted in Him. And He, again, honors us and rewards us Himself, acknowledging us as wise. Again, such beautiful

Words. This all points us to His Great Commission and our part in His calling us. He shows us in these verses and Words to us, too, that in our own coming to Jesus for salvation and forgiveness for our sins, there were trees planted for us. And from those trees we plucked and ate. From this fruit of the trees, of those who were and are still righteous, He brought us to salvation. He is, according to His Word, already prospering those who answered His call. Prospering those who bore fruit which led others to salvation. And so, with each of us, trees which will bear fruit for Him to use to lead others to salvation.

Father, I pray, help us not let our fruit rot on our branches. But be plucked by those who are hungry and can be forever satisfied by it and the life, eternal life, it will bring to them as they eat!!!

Alleluia!!!Ghost Writer For God

Laura Russell Simpson 2-28-16

ON PRAYER AND PRAISE

Remember as you pray to offer up praise and thanksgiving to God! We should always worship as we seek Him and His help, whatever our requests are.

Alleluia!!!

Ghost Writer For God
Laura Russell Simpson

A PRAYER FOR GOD'S PEOPLE AS WE PRAY FOR OUR NATION

2 Chronicles 7:14

If My people, which are called by My name, shall humble themselves, and pray, and seek My face, and turn from their wicked ways; then will I hear from Heaven, and will forgive their sin, and heal their land.

My friends, who are fellow Christians, Our God is speaking to us! Would you join me now in this prayer for our great nation, which God gave to us?

Our Father, who art in Heaven,

We, Your people, come humbly before You, confessing our sins against You, both individually and collectively. We seek Your forgiveness for turning away from You and following false gods. This day we turn back to You. In thanksgiving to You as our God and in thanksgiving for the truth of Your Word and Your great faithfulness, we call upon Your great Name and ask You to heal our land. We acknowledge that we cannot do this on our own. We must have Your help. Thy will be done on earth as it is in Heaven. We offer up these prayers with our praises and worship to the One who alone is Worthy to be praised!!!

Alleluia!!!

Ghost Writer for God
Laura Russell Simpson 8-12-17

THE MIRACLE OF GOD'S LOVE AND HOW HE ENABLES US TO LOVE THE UNLOVELY

Galatians 5:22&23

But the fruit of the Spirit is love, joy, peace, long suffering, gentleness, goodness, faith, meekness, and temperance: against such there is no law.

Galatians 5:25

If we live in the Spirit, let us also walk in the Spirit.

There is not one of us who has not faced the conflict of loving someone who is unlovely, someone who has mistreated us or has hurt us in some way. Each of us knows how difficult this can be. But God has a way to make this happen. And His way of enabling us to love the unlovely is found in these two verses in Galatians. Through my own personal experience and testimony, I am able to say that what He has revealed to me as His truth, He has also proved once again His faithfulness to His Word. Simply put, if we follow His Word, we will experience love for those who are unlovely, love for those who have mistreated us, and love for those who have hurt us. Again, I know this to be true, because I have lived it. In Galatians 5:25 we are told, if we live in the Spirit, we are to walk in the Spirit. This is the key. At our salvation experience we are given the Holy Spirit, who takes up residence in us. Please note here We are given the Holy Spirit of Almighty God! His Word tells us these bodies, though flesh, are the temple of the Holy Spirit (1Corithians 6:19). However, we are also told we can quench and grieve the Holy Spirit(1Thessalonians 5:19) (Ephesians 4:30). Over a period of time, if we do quench, and or, grieve Him He will withdraw from us. This happens, not because He leaves us, but because we leave Him, pulling away by choosing to walk in the flesh. Note here, also, this is a choice we make. It is vital that we choose to walk in the Spirit, and not according to the flesh. If we do not, then the miracle of God's love will not happen in us. Our very own choice will stop it. The great news for us is that, if we do walk in the Spirit, we will experience the fruit which He produces in our lives. This is a gift God gives us, not something we can produce in ourselves. It will come and come quite naturally in us. And remember here that it is fruit, not fruits, even though there are many parts of His fruit. The part of His fruit, God reveals to us here, which enables us to love the unlovely is the first one given. And that one is LOVE! In our flesh, and because of our weakness, we cannot love the unlovely on our own. We simply cannot produce this love in ourselves. But as we walk in the Holy Spirit, the fruit of His love in us will enable us to love the unlovely, those who have mistreated or hurt us. This love comes from God alone and will come quite naturally to and through us. We will see and experience the miracle of God's love as we see Him reveal this in those we want to love. It will happen and, again, quite naturally. We do not have to strive any longer, trying on our own or in our flesh. He will make it happen. His love will flow in and through us to others. A beautiful by-product of this is true forgiveness. When He gives us this love, we will also soon realize that our hearts will be full of His love, but, also, full of forgiveness for those we have wanted to love and to forgive. Again, it is a miracle from a loving and forgiving God for all. What He knows we cannot do in ourselves, He will graciously do for us. He knew we could not deliver ourselves from sin, so He delivered us by the gift of His Son and the blood Jesus shed on Calvary's cross. And in this, lesson we see He will deliver us, also, from the bondages of hate and bitterness we hold toward those who have offended us. Please note here, God delivers us. We cannot deliver ourselves. Another grand display of His awesome love and forgiveness, which He so very much wants to give us and to enable us to have for others. Yes, my friends, a true miracle of the love of God in our hearts! And where there is love, there is forgiveness. And where there is forgiveness, there is freedom!!! And where there is freedom, there is peace. And where there is peace, there is joy!!!

Alleluia!!!

Ghost Writer For God
Laura Russell Simpson 2-16-16

MORE ON THE MIRACLE OF GOD'S LOVE AND HOW HE ENABLES US TO LOVE THE UNLOVELY

It, again, is all about choice. God shows us in the very beginning in the book of Genesis that He gave Adam and Eve a choice. They could either eat the fruit of the forbidden tree or not. And do not miss the significance of the word fruit. The fruit they chose to eat caused their spirits and bodies to die. God shows us, clearly, we have a choice. The first one we make is the Way of salvation, God's way and the only Way. At salvation, we choose Jesus as Savior, but we also have the choice of making Him Lord of our lives. If we make Him Lord, we crucify self and follow Him. It is the Holy Spirit who enables us to follow Him. The fruit of the flesh, when we are struggling to love the unlovely is anger, bitterness, hate, resentment, and on and on. And the results will lead only to misery and defeat. But the fruit of the spirit is love, joy, peace, long suffering, gentleness, goodness, faith, meekness, and temperance. And this is God's supernatural way of enabling us to live in love, forgiveness, joy, victory and freedom. To mention just one other example is the part of this fruit, the part of peace. Remember His Words to be anxious for nothing, but in everything through prayer and supplication with thanksgiving, let your requests be made known to God, and the peace of God which surpasses all understanding will keep your hearts and minds in Christ Jesus. Look closely here. He offers us His supernatural peace, and that supernatural peace will keep our hearts and minds in Christ Jesus. We could go on to look at other parts of His fruit and see this same message to us. But we close here. My friends, can you see the great love of our Father for each of us? And how He shares with us through the fruit of His Holy Spirit. But it comes with a choice. My prayer is for each of us to choose His Way and truly live in joy, victory, and freedom that Christ's shed blood won for us on Calvary's cross. God's Word says that sin no longer has dominion over us. In this message, again, He shows us the way out and reveals Himself and the truth of His Word. Let us walk in His love, empowered by His Holy

Spirit and enjoy our life this side of eternity! It is ours for the receiving!!!

Alleluia!!!

Ghost Writer For God
Laura Russell Simpson 2-16-16

A FINAL WORD ON HATE

My friends, the message here, again, is God's deliverance. At the cross God delivered us through the shed blood of our Savior, Jesus Christ. But His deliverance goes far beyond the cross. It continues to reach down and deliver us again and again. He sees our helplessness, and always, as we look to Him, He proves Himself over and over!!!

Alleluia!!!

Ghost Writer For God
Laura Russell Simpson 2-23-16

BE ENCOURAGED

Jesus says what He does. And He does what He says! I give testimony to this truth. And this truth lives in me, as I walk with Him. We just have to call upon Him. He will always be there for us! When our faith is weak, let us ask Him to take us to a place where we believe beyond our faith, and watch Him as He works in our lives and in proving Himself true to His promises, thus moving us to a much greater faith. His gift to us!!!

Alleluia!!!

Ghost Writer For God
Laura Russell Simpson 2-29-16

GOD'S HELP FOR US IN PRAYING FOR OUR CHILDREN

Numbers 6:22-27

And the Lord spake unto Moses, saying, speak unto Aaron and his sons, saying unto them, the Lord bless thee and keep thee: the Lord make His face to shine upon thee, and be gracious unto thee: the Lord lift up His countenance upon thee, and give thee peace. And they shall put My name upon the children of Israel; and I will bless them.

This is a passage that we probably all have heard many times. But what is so awesome is the last verse, verse 27. In this verse, there is a great promise, a promise to bless our children, our grandchildren and future generations. He is saying to us if we put His name upon our children, He will bless them! He wants us to speak His name upon them, to pray over them and proclaim His name over them. When we do this, the results will be God's blessings over them and their lives. Because His name is placed upon them, they will be His. He will bring them to Himself, teach them, reveal Himself to them, carry them through their life journey, always drawing them close to Himself. As we do what God tells us here, we do not have to worry about our children. Standing in faith, believing Him and His Words of promise, we will never be discouraged or fearful for our children. Even when their lives do not reflect what we want for them, we can be assured that their steps are ordered, their days fashioned by their Creator, before He ever lent them to us. We have His promise because we are His children. His name is upon us and we, too, can bring blessings upon our precious ones by placing our God and Father's name upon them, calling each one by name. As God's children, because of our being in Christ, we are joint heirs with Him. So, let us place His name upon those He has given us and pass down our inheritance to them. Let us proclaim them His! And wait and watch for His blessings on them. As a result, too, we will be blessed even more! Remember, He is ALWAYS faithful to His Words of promise!!!

Alleluia!!!

Ghost Writer For God
Laura Russell Simpson 4-3-16

Do not let the enemy of our souls take you to the "what ifs". Let God take you there, even if He does! If He then does, He will be there with you in the "what ifs", too. He will NEVER leave you or forsake you, even in the "what ifs"!!!

Alleluia!!!

Ghost Writer For God
Laura Russell Simpson

Hebrews 13:5.......for He hath said, I will never leave thee nor forsake thee.

ON PENTECOST AND REVIVAL

Acts 2:1-4

And when the day of Pentecost was fully come, they were all in one accord in one place. And suddenly there came a sound from Heaven as of a rushing mighty wind, and it filled all the house where they were sitting. And there appeared unto them cloven tongues like as of fire, and it sat upon each of them. And they were filled with the Holy Ghost, and began to speak with other tongues, as the Spirit gave them utterance.

Again, God wants to speak to us about His Holy Spirit. And He wants us to understand the importance of Pentecost in true revival, and the vital part that the Holy Spirit is in both Pentecost and true revival. It grieves Him that so many are afraid of His Holy Spirit. Also, it grieves Him that His church has fallen short on teaching His truth about

His Spirit. Where the Holy Spirit is not welcomed or invited, there is no life. And no power or fruit. This is true not only for His church, but for us personally. True revival begins in us individually in our own hearts. Then that leads to us as His church and on to others. The Holy Spirit first came at Pentecost. It was at that time that they were empowered to go forth and preach the Gospel to all the world. Notice here the Holy Spirit came with great sound and power, and it came from Heaven, sent by God. Important to see here is that His presence filled all the house. Then there came the cloven tongues like a fire. And it says that these cloven tongues sat upon each of them. God's revelation here is that it was with the tongues of fire that they would go forth and preach the Gospel message to all the world. God was giving them the source of power to speak boldly and powerfully to a lost world. It is with the tongue we speak. And it is not by coincidence that this part of the body He touched with fire power. Very important next is that the Holy Spirit sat upon each one individually, not as a group. The Spirit then filled all of them with His presence. They then spoke in other tongues guided by the Spirit. This passage goes on to tell us that because of this each one from every nation heard them speak in their own language. Important to note here is that people from every nation experienced Pentecost. It was at this day that God birthed His church, which brings us to the present time and His message to us, His people, on a personal "PENTECOST". And this will only come by the work of the Holy Spirit, first in our own hearts and then, collectively, as His church. True revival will never happen without the Holy Spirit. We need to repent of our sin of quenching His Spirit and seek a fresh touch, a renewal, a revival from God. We need to give His Spirit the freedom to do His work in us and then through us. With that will come empowerment and then boldness from tongues touched with fire power to go forth in our day and share the Gospel message to a lost world, just as at the day of Pentecost! As we experience our own personal "Pentecost", revival will begin and then spread. Remember here that this presence and empowerment was given to all peoples of all nations! But notice that on that day, the Holy Spirit sat upon each one individually first. Thus, God shows us the importance of our own "Pentecost" experience before we can experience true revival. And, again, that will never come without the work of His Holy Spirit!

Alleluia!!!

Ghost Writer For God: Laura Russell Simpson 6-12-16

GIVING THANKS AND PRAISE TO
THE ONE WHO IS WORTHY

Psalm 139:14

……..marvelous are Thy works; and that my soul knoweth right well.

Alleluia!!!

Ghost Writer For God
Laura Russell Simpson 6-17-16

A STRONG WARNING FROM GOD

Acts 12:23

And immediately the angel of the Lord smote him, because he gave not God the glory: and he was eaten of worms, and gave up the ghost.

Colossians 1:27

......which is Christ in you, the hope of glory.

God wants us to clearly see the seriousness of giving the glory, that belongs to Him alone, to another! His message is very strong as you see in this scripture. We must never esteem another above God. Respect, yes, but never esteem. When we begin to look at someone and begin to esteem them, we are setting them up for a fall. God will NEVER share His glory with any man or woman! That person will, by the hand of God, fall before our very eyes. We all will always fall, disappoint, and sin in many ways. He wants us to see the truth of this and be sensitive to what will inevitably happen to that one we fall prey to esteeming above Him. And never should any of us esteem ourselves! He will not allow this at any time. WE are always to acknowledge Him as the source of all we have. And the recipient of all glory! Everything we do should glorify God. He alone is worthy of our praises and glory! In the second scripture, it is Christ in us our hope of glory. Notice here that Christ in us is our hope of glory, not what we have now, but our hope of what is to come. And that will come only through having Christ in us. We have no hope of anything without having Christ in us. He is the reason we have hope! And what a glorious hope we have, now and also to come. In closing, I believe that giving another the glory that belongs only to God may be one of our most grievous sins against God. The evidence of this is given in the scripture from Acts.

Father, help us to always be mindful of giving You the glory that belongs only to You. And in doing so, we will protect ourselves and others from falling.

Alleluia!!!

Ghost Writer For God
Laura Russell Simpson 4-26-16

ON VICTORY

Romans 6:14

For sin shall not have dominion over you.

If you are going through a dark time, remember that, if you belong to Him, the victory is yours! Jesus won our victory on the cross. Satan was defeated, and God tells us in His Word that sin no longer has dominion over us. Our victory flag might drop to half- mast when we are going through tough times, but it will rise again to the top! One of God's seven names is God Our Banner. It is God who goes before us! He carries the victory flag, and the battle is His! The darkness will give way to His light, and we will soon watch our flag rise again to the top. My friends, do not be discouraged! Stand strong in your faith, trusting Him and looking up to Him, waiting patiently for Him to complete His work, and when it is time, the darkness will move over and your flag will rise again! God then speaks!!! What He shows us in all this is that because of the darkness our vision became blurred. We could not see that the flag of victory was never at half-mast! Because of our discouragement, it just appeared that way. Remembering again that the victory was won at the cross by our Savior, Jesus Christ! That has not and will not ever change!!! God's own Words, "It is Finished"! My friends, His victory is ours, too!!!

Alleluia!!!

Ghost Writer For God
Laura Russell Simpson 5-17-16

CALMING OUR STORMS

Mark 4:35-41

And the same day, when the even was come, He saith unto them, Let us pass over to the other side. And when they had sent away the multitude, they took Him even as he was in the ship. And there were also with Him other little ships. And there arose a great storm of wind, and the waves beat into the ship, so that it was now full. And He was in the hinder part of the ship, asleep on a pillow; and they awake Him, and say unto Him, Master, caress Thou not that we perish? And he arose, and rebuked the wind, and said unto the sea, Peace, be still. And the wind ceased, and there was a great calm. And He said unto them, Why are ye so fearful? How is that ye have no faith? And they feared exceedingly, and said one to another, What manner of man is this, that even the wind and the sea obey him?

In verse 35 notice it was evening, growing dark. Jesus is leading them in the dark into a storm. Look what He says. He is also getting ready to take them through the storm to the other side to a place He has already chosen for them. And He is going with them. He says, let us pass. So, they are not going to be alone in this storm. He will be with them. Look here at the personal application in this one verse. He speaks this to us, also. Notice in verse 36 that there were other smaller ships with them. Others were going to go through this storm, too. Those, also, would experience what He was going to do. Same thing with us. There are many who share our storms. And some of those may be just the ones we are battling with in our storm. They are going to experience His miracle, also. We all need Him and His power and miracles in our storms. Just like all the other boats, we are all needy. In verse 37 the storm comes, full force. The boat becomes full of water. Same, again, with us. Our storms become hurricane strength at times and, yes, our boats fill up with water, too. Notice the disciples did nothing until the boat was full, except panic. Why did they not awake Him before the boat was full of water? Do we see ourselves in this? In verse 38 Jesus is asleep on a pillow when they awake Him. Their question to Him is, do You not care that we are perishing? What God is showing us here is that Jesus was asleep on a pillow for two reasons. First, He is on a pillow, comfortable. The storm did not intimidate Him. And secondly, Jesus was waiting on them to ask for His help, to turn to Him in their time of need. Same message for us! We wait too long before we seek His help when we are in a hard place. We follow the same path as given in this passage. We question whether He cares. In verse 39 Jesus arises, rebukes the wind and speaks to the sea. His words are, Peace, be still! The wind and sea obey. Look what happens next. And there was a great calm. Not just a calm, but a great calm! Total peace. And notice here the storm stops. And so, will ours. Our storms do end and when they end, we, too, have peace and calmness, great calmness! In verse 40 He asks us, just as He asked His disciples, in the darkness of their storm that night, Why do we fear? We do not have to be afraid in our storms, either. And He asks us, too, how is it that we have no faith? Can you not hear and feel His disappointment in their fear and total lack of faith? Same with us. We hurt our Lord when we do not trust Him, knowing the power He has to take us through our appointed storms. Like that night, Jesus will remain "asleep on His pillow" until we seek Him and His help. And when we do "awaken" Him, there will be great calm in our lives!!! It is Jesus who can and will rebuke our storms. And in closing, we will be like His disciples that night, too, looking at Him in awe, amazed at His power and even fearful, because we have experienced the Lord Jesus Christ!!!

Alleluia!!!

Ghost Writer For God, Laura Russell Simpson 4-25-16

OUR PRAYER TO GOD

Father, we humbly ask. Help us not block our own blessings!

In Jesus Name,

Ghost Writer For God
Laura Russell Simpson 8-14-17

GOD'S WONDERFUL WORDS ON HIS HELP TO US IN OUR INFIRMITIES

2 Corinthians 12:9

And He said unto me, My grace is sufficient for thee: for My strength is made perfect in weakness. Most gladly therefore will I glory in my infirmities, that the power of Christ may rest upon me.

God's message to us through the words He gave to the apostle, Paul, are powerful, comforting and so very, very true. He tells us right away that His grace is all we need. And it is important to hear, as He speaks, first to us about His grace. It is this grace that flows throughout this scripture. Then in our weakness His strength comes to us. We are not left alone in times of weakness. He comes to us and brings us His strength. This kind of strength belongs only to Him. But through this, because of His grace, He does not leave us on our own. Again, we see that it is sufficient.

It is truly all we need. How beautiful is that? Paul now speaks of glorying in his infirmities. What this says, he does not glory because of his infirmities, but in them. This is significant. In his glory, Paul is glorifying God because God has shown him the truth of this message. Paul sees, as he has lived it, that in these times, the very power of Christ will come and literally rest upon him. His words are words of praise and worship to God. And listen carefully. His power, which comes here to us, will rest upon us, also. Do you hear God's Words as they bring us comfort and help and a release from our struggles? This rest comes, too, only from God. It is, in Christ, that we experience this supernatural rest. And that is only His, too. I close with praise and thanksgiving to our wonderful Father and our Savior, Jesus Christ, and His Holy Spirit, who has revealed another great truth of His Word! We simply must not ignore His Word, because, if we do, we will live in defeat, despair, hopelessness, and misery. God's love and grace is always ours!!! He shows us the way of salvation first, then the way of true peace, true joy, victory and help. Let us walk in the truth and power of His Word!!!

Alleluia!!!

Ghost Writer For God
Laura Russell Simpson 2-23-16

ON FOREVER

And He shall reign forever, and forever, and forever,
until there is no forever, He still will reign!!!

Alleluia!!!

Ghost Writer For God
Laura Russell Simpson 8-14-17

ABOUT THE AUTHOR

Laura Russell Simpson is in reality the ghost writer for the One who gave her these teachings, namely, Almighty God. She is one whose life has been dramatically changed by the power of Almighty God. After years of struggles through pits and prisons, like Joseph, the patriarch, God has now brought her out to an abundant life of victory and joy, no matter the circumstances. Her heart's desire is to serve the God she loves, first by answering His call to share His great love for all, to share the way of salvation through His Son, Jesus Christ, and to share the truth and power of His Word, which she highly esteems. She resides with her husband, Bill, in her hometown of Rock Hill, South Carolina, and has been blessed with a daughter, Lauran, and a grandson, Josh. She considers herself to be greatly blessed by the God she loves, and lovingly serves.